Presented To

Sharon & Dana

In Memory Of

Muffin

By

Lin & Julie Van Nest & Kids

Date

11/18/04

Happiness is a warm puppy.

—Charles Schulz

I still miss you...

Letters of Comfort for Dog Lovers

A Veterinarian Shares His Stories

DR. JACK TITOLO D.V.M.

I Still Miss You: Letters of Comfort for Dog Lovers
ISBN 1-59475-014-9
Copyright © 2003 by Jack Titolo, D.V.M.
Copyright © 2003 by GRQ Ink, Inc.
Published by Blue Sky Ink, Brentwood, Tennessee

All letters are based on actual notes sent to pet owners by Dr. Jack,
with names changed and contents altered to protect privacy.

Editor: Lila Empson
Compiler: Richard C. Lawrence
Cover and interior design:
    Whisner Group, Tulsa, Oklahoma
Printed in China

What feeling do we ever find

to equal among humankind

a dog's fidelity!

—Thomas Hardy

Contents

Introduction

When I watch species other than my own,
their instinct's wisdom is what most impresses
and disturbs me.

—Charles A. Lindbergh

$\mathcal{I}$ have spent most of my life with dogs. As a boy growing up in America's rural heartland, I learned early that animals could be my most reliable companions. I had lots of pets—cats, a turtle, even a raccoon—but the deepest relationships, the ones I keep returning to in my mind, were with dogs. Riding my bike down a two-lane road, fishing in a shady stream on a summer afternoon, hiking through shin-deep snow—how much less memorable, less meaningful, they all would have been without the English setter at my side!

Early on, I decided I would make my profession that of caring for these creatures. And a funny thing happened: As I gained experience, and watched dogs with their owners, I began to realize that the dogs were caring for the humans as much as vice versa.

As a veterinarian, I have witnessed the sadness of having to let go of a pet, and I have also experienced it as a dog owner. I consider it a privilege to be able to show caring during a pet's last moments. It is because of this unique intimacy that I have written these letters of explanation and encouragement.

Jack Titolo, DVM

A Dog's-Eye View of Human Ownership

The better I get to know men, the more I find myself loving dogs.

—Charles de Gaulle

Dogs and humans have been partners for at least ten thousand years. There is no relationship quite like this one. It transcends explanation. Our dogs make us feel special, complete. I believe they are given to us to change our hearts—to make us better, more loving, more compassionate people. The deepest part of ourselves is touched by their wordless depths. No one can put a value on this bond that ties the fabric of who we are.

Humans have shaped dogs, literally. The range of physical variation in *Canis familiaris* is astounding, from the Great Dane to the Chihuahua, from the sled-pulling malamute to the lap-sitting toy poodle, from the shaggy sheepdog to the Mexican hairless. The American Kennel Club recognizes 137 breeds. If dogs were human, they'd have an identity crisis. But being dogs, they know who they are, who we are, and what they're for.

If they could talk, collies and shepherds would say, "I want to herd sheep!" Spaniels, hounds, and terriers would say, "I want to hunt!" Dobermans would say, "I want to guard this house!" What dogs want most from humans is to be given the tasks they were bred for. The gratifications humans seek from pets—companionship, loyalty, affection, exercise—come easiest when the dogs' natures are fulfilled.

Yes, many dog breeds were formed for work—but that alone can't explain the special human-canine bond. Watch a dog at work sometime. A dog is not a drudge, an unwilling employee marking time. A dog is a fiery, fleshly spirit, alive with the joy of performing its proper task. (In this, dogs can teach us much.) And when the dog's job is simply to be a companion, the dog goes at it with all the zeal, the love, the gusto, of a bloodhound chasing prey, a cattle dog corralling calves, or a guide dog navigating for his sightless friend.

One reason dogs love humans so is that dogs are pack animals. The larger breeds see us as "top dog." Their plea to their human leader is, "Tell me what to do, and I'll do it!" Smaller breeds often see us as top dog, too—except that they still see some hope for making us trainable!

Good-Bye, Faithful Friend

When a beautiful and affectionate dog leaves this world, the owner keenly feels a hollow space inside. Perhaps the dog lived long and comfortably, dying peacefully overnight. Or perhaps the dog fell to disease in youth or middle age, was struck by a car or shot in a hunting accident, or was snatched away by human criminality. The particulars may vary, but the honor due a faithful dog's life does not vary. The loss of a dog, whether after fifteen months or fifteen years, is a shock, and the owner is deeply grieved.

There are three stages to this final parting. The first is *preparation*. You know the time is coming. The day comes when you can't think of anything else. Then, you reach the second stage, *departure*. This is the actual scene of leave-taking. The final stage is *grief*. Mourning takes you from initial shock to ultimate acceptance.

In cases of terminal illness or crippling injury, many owners choose to euthanize a dog to spare it unnecessary suffering. I believe that when you accept the pain of grief to spare your pet the pain of lingering illness, you are demonstrating unselfish love. People who make this sacrifice deserve our comfort and support.

Remembering the Joy

In time, the ache softens. Somehow, mysteriously, through time's healing power, painful memories diminish and happy ones return to the forefront. We look at photos of our furry friends—running after sticks, jumping to catch balls, sitting up to beg for treats, giving our children rides. We watch videos and laugh at old pranks even more heartily than when they were new. We retell stories of our lost companions, smiling.

The intensity of grief can last hours, days, even years. A bereaved dog owner may recognize his or her dog in everything—a chair, a ball, a bowl of water. And each new visitation of memory may be accompanied by cleansing tears. Years later, in a private, unseen, intimate room in the heart, an odor, a sight, or a sound might trigger a twinge of recaptured loss. Safely tucked away in that special place are memories of the beloved companion, always ready for a visit, never to be lost again.

In my experience, grief can lead us to become more compassionate and more loving. Going through the process from denial to acceptance can enrich one's appreciation of life, and this understanding can be our dogs' last and lasting gift to us.

The dog was created especially for children. He is the god of frolic.
—Henry Ward Beecher

A Lesson from Steinbeck and His Dad

Veterinarians don't just take care of animals. We must know how to care for people, too. Here's just one example of what I mean, from my files and my memory.

Steinbeck was a standard poodle cross, and Mr. Bordland brought him in for all his shots and treatments. When Steinbeck showed early signs of kidney disease in middle age, Mr. Bordland assured me he would go to any lengths to restore his friend's health. In my office we discussed treatment plans. He leaned his head into his open palms.

"I've never had children," he said. "That is, Steinbeck is my child. He means so much to me, and his love is the purest I've ever seen. He goes with me everywhere. We go on five-mile hikes on weekends, and I even talked the owner of my office building into letting me keep him at work. He would die for me; I know he would."

It was hard for me to watch Mr. Bordland try not to cry, but I understood what he was going through. Earlier in my career, I might have seen my role as only that of treating Steinbeck. Now I know better. Almost as important, I was there for Steinbeck's dad.

Fondly,

Dr. Jack

You can't teach old fleas new dogs.
—Federico Fellini

Almond Joy

Dear Mr. and Mrs. Stark,

We first saw Almond Joy fourteen years ago in the spring, a frolicsome seventeen-and-a-half-pound Dalmatian youngster. She must have been a handful, because only two weeks later she was in with a sprained left front leg. Once you were worried she had glass in her paws, but it turned out to be loose kneecaps. She had the usual assortment of coughs, throw-ups, surprise pregnancies, head tilting, bad breath, you name it. At one time she had back problems. This is what we knew about her, and yet it's a small perspective. Outside this clinic, she probably owned your home.

This spring, however, her intervertebral disk disease was visibly progressing, dooming her to a pain-riddled, weakened old age. You faced a hard choice, and you made the right one. I have twenty-four pages of records to prove what good parents you were. And I have the memory of Mrs. Stark's treatment-room eulogy: "Good-bye my beautiful girl, who never hurt anyone."

You've had other dogs, but each is unique, and each had a special place in your lives. Now it's time for this one to take her rightful place in your hearts—forever.

Take heart,

Dr. Jack

I can remember when he was a pup.
—Robert Frost

Biscuit

Dear Ms. McIntosh,

A week ago today, you brought Biscuit in. There is little anyone can say to ease your grief, but here are my thoughts. She was a paradox—an Australian cattle dog, a breed known for its toughness and strong fortitude, and yet you named her Biscuit, a name suggesting cuteness and lightness. Biscuit was a sweetheart, and even with so much hair missing, she was still beautiful. And don't let that name fool anyone. She'd spend all day patrolling her yard, keeping its borders safe.

When she started losing that much weight for no apparent reason, we knew something was very wrong. I can tell you this: She didn't suffer. Her lymphoma had spread quickly and with little pain. She probably felt feverish and lethargic, like she had the flu the last couple of days.

I was deeply moved by your unselfishness in letting Biscuit go. She was your family for more than a decade. I smile when I remember that you can still see the mark she made when she chewed on your dining chair leg. What we wouldn't give to see her chewing on that leg again!

Take heart, and remember the wonderful years you had with Biscuit.

With good memories,

Dr. Jack

A dog has one aim in life. To bestow his heart.

—J. R. Ackerley

Rutherford

*D*ear Mr. Grant,

Sometimes when we grieve the loss of a pet, the emptiness seems unbearable. Rutherford lived long and fully. He survived heartworm in 1995, and did pretty well until this last year. He was a tough old dog, but because of his age, his bodily functions and mental acuity were breaking down. Eventually he would have had little dignity left. I know you miss him, but you did right to let him go. Take heart in the lovingness of your decision.

Sincerely,

Dr. Jack

Dogs give their human companions unconditional love and are always there with an encouraging wag of the tail when they are needed. The dog is indeed a very special animal.

—Dorothy Hinshaw Patent

Natasha

Dear Mr. and Mrs. Martinson,

With all that's happened in Natasha's life, it's a blessing she was with you as long she was. I've been reviewing her record. What a history that little cocker spaniel had! She first came to us in November 1987. She weighed five and a half pounds and came in for puppy shots. Since then, she virtually had to have her own file cabinet, she'd been in so much between her epilepsy and heart problems—a total of fifty visits exactly. When healthy, she was full of kisses and mischief. But her little heart started having trouble in July 1999, and after four more years, it just couldn't go anymore.

I know how hard it is to say good-bye to our little furry creatures. I've had to do it twice in my life and thought I was going to die of heartbreak both times. You were good parents and gave Natasha the best care possible. In your eyes, she could do no wrong. Small mistakes were quickly forgiven, and she returned love to you as only a canine can.

Your last day with her was also your kindest day. You were there, and she was ready. She'll be missed.

Be encouraged,

Dr. Jack

The question is not, Can they reason? nor, Can they talk?, but, Can they suffer?

—Jeremy Bentham

Jamie

$\mathcal{D}$ear Mr. and Mrs. Custis,

Your little dachshund was one big fighter. Last month he was so thin and weary that most dogs would have given up right then. But he wanted to live. He never once tried to fight us or lash out at us when we placed his IV line or gave him antibiotics. But he just ran out of life. Acute pancreatitis is one of the more complicated diseases that can befall a well-cared-for, middle-aged dog like Jamie.

When healthy, Jamie was a joy. The exam room would be different because he was there. He could look at you and be happy or disgusted—and it mattered. That's the way dachshunds are. They amuse us with their appearance, but they are hardworking, intelligent creatures, first bred for hunting badgers in tunnels, who take serious joy in doing their best.

When you came in the front door of the clinic that day, holding Jamie panting and whimpering in your arms, I could tell that you knew you would not be carrying him out again. We can't undo life's end. All I can do is let you know that I grieve with you, and I'm here to talk with you.

Thinking of you all,

Dr. Jack

If you pick up a starving dog and make him prosperous, he will not bite you. This is the principal difference between a man and a dog.
—Mark Twain

Shade

$\mathcal{D}$ear Bill and Susie,

We are grieved to hear of Shade's passing. He was a dirty gray stray in that springtime four years ago. Boy, did he pick the right house. He came to you complete with fleas, malnourishment, and heartworm. You took him in, fed him, had him treated, and spent months helping rehabilitate his hips. Now, in Shade's season of strength, a careless driver crashed through an innocent afternoon romp.

Nothing could surpass your goodness to animals. Keep going, and be brave.

Fondly,

Dr. Jack

At night, when all was quiet about the campfire, [Stickeen] would come to me and rest his head on my knee with a look of devotion as if I were his god.

—John Muir

29

Jenkins

Dear Mr. Mayhew,

I received your note about Jenkins's sudden stroke—and I grieve with you. As his vet and friend, I always saw Jenkins's great love for you in the way he looked at you. It was as if he was saying, "I want to be with you, I want to play, but I just can't make these legs work fast enough. I can't get enough air when I breathe. I hurt and I don't know why." He had no idea what "old" was. He only knew he wasn't the first one up in the morning anymore. And he was so tired.

Jenkins woke each day with a job to do: to see you and your family through the seasons, the years, the passages of life. Your children grew up with Jenkins, from the first nervous walk to kindergarten, to happy roughhousing in cap-and-gown on graduation day. There were shopping trips with a dog yipping in the backseat, and garage sales on Saturday mornings. Jenkins barked a lot, knocked over things with his wagging tail, even managed to get hit in the head with an ax once—fortunately, the blunt side! In the end, he was perfect for your family. And in memory, he still is.

Take courage,

Dr. Jack

The dog was created especially for children. He is the god of frolic.
—Henry Ward Beecher

Mack

*D*ear Mrs. Portman,

Just a few lines to tell you that the autopsy shows no doubt—Mack succumbed to cancer. At Mack's stage of illness, no amount of medication or treatment would have done more than prolong his suffering.

Mack's life had a terrible start when he lost his leg, having been shot by a hunter before he was even two years old. But he was tough. He made it through and lived eight more years. So somebody—you—did something right. You worked with him and cheered him on while facing your own struggles. You cared for his happiness but didn't let him indulge in just anything. You knew what was good for him. And I suspect that during his struggles, Mack sensed your ups and down as much as his own.

My wife and I enjoyed visiting you occasionally for the sheer pleasure of watching a Doberman with three legs run like the wind. On Mack's last day, she was grieving for him when I came home for dinner. She had heard the news of his passing, and, as you know, she loved him too.

It's good you have others to care for. I know that each of these creatures is unique—Mack left an empty space that your other pets can't fill. But hang in there and be encouraged.

Be of good heart,

Dr. Jack

I'd rather have an inch of dog than miles of pedigree.
—Dana Burnet

Viscount

Dear Mr. and Mrs. Gottesman,

When I first saw Viscount all those years ago, he was a skinny little orphan with mites and fleas. You spruced him up and tended to him through more than his share of problems. He was on thyroid medicine since anyone can remember. At twelve, he developed chronic kidney problems. Even so, he lived four more years. He must have had a heart for living—that, and good care. It takes both. You deserve credit for giving him a good life.

Best wishes,

Dr. Jack

The great pleasure of a dog is that you may make a fool of yourself with him and not only will he not scold you, but he will make a fool of himself too.

—Samuel Butler

Colonel

*D*ear Mr. and Mrs. Forbes,

I knew there was something special about Colonel when I first saw him. He was a handsome, crop-eared, white-chested boxer, and a family dog from the start. His greatest joy was to be around you. He just wanted his family. He was a good wrestler, a good protector, and a good companion. He could beg a steak off the table, but he knew his place. If it can be said that a dog could have honor, he had it, and a well-bred gentleness. He never complained about what we had to do, and without fuss he withstood biopsy, surgery, and radiation therapy for his melanoma. Even on the examining table, he was easy to love and accepted affection readily.

When I met both of you, I knew where Colonel's special quality came from. His gentle strength was a manifestation of your own, and his responsiveness was the fruit of your caring.

We could not reverse the course of his cancer, but we could prevent further pain from debilitating him. I could see love and pain in your eyes when this cruel disease struck Colonel down in the prime of life. He'll be missed. He was a star.

Truly,

Dr. Jack

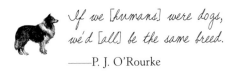

If we [humans] were dogs, we'd [all] be the same breed.

——P. J. O'Rourke

Lenny

*D*ear Mr. and Mrs. Thomson,

By this time, life without stalwart little Lenny must be setting in. Lenny was a loyal friend to you since puphood, a well-trained, obedient Welsh corgi whose greatest pride was protecting his family. Your children never knew life without him. I remember you telling me how he once kept you up all night yapping at the edge of his invisible fence. Next morning, you found a prowler's glove in the driveway—but your home and belongings were intact.

But at age fifteen, he was in end-stage heart failure. His heart murmur was first noticed six months ago. That's three years in human time. Dogs just don't live as long as we do, and they age several times quicker. The disease progressed remorselessly. We could have performed a number of diagnostics and pressed ahead with various treatments, but the reality of the situation was that Lenny would have succumbed to his disease. He was worthy of the benevolent release you allowed him.

Lenny had a bad heart, but in another sense he had a lot of heart—a large spirit in a little body, who impacted your lives with loyalty and faithfulness. I know he is greatly missed.

Take courage,

Dr. Jack

There is no faith which has never yet been broken, except that of a truly faithful dog.
—Konrad Lorenz

Bud

Dear Jimmy,

This world can be so unfair. Losing a friend can tear you up—especially unexplained loss to an unknown assailant. Bud was so handsome, they should have made a breed out of him. There's always hope, but after six months I think we need to accept that he was stolen and is gone. All of us who have given our hearts to dogs are with you and your parents this day. Come in and talk whenever you feel like it.

Take care,

Dr. Jack

A dog gets lonesome just like a human.
He wants to associate with other dogs,
but when they take him out,
the poor dog is on a leash and
cannot run around.

—Langston Hughes

Marion

Dear Ms. Minghella,

Marion was so good, she didn't even whimper. I carried her, thin and rapid-pulsed, into the treatment room. Here was the dog you and I have pulled out of so many jams in the past. We always knew we'd be facing this day, especially with a heart as bad as hers. Frankly, Afghans aren't known for longevity. But because you were a good mom, she was able to live a quality life till age thirteen.

We discovered her heart problem back in September of last year. In January it was minus 15 degrees outside, and she was hospitalized for hypothermia. She bounced back from that. Then we almost lost her last month and back she came. She didn't know what "give up" meant.

As hard as all this was for her, I think it was even harder on you. Toward the end I know you were thinking about her leaving you every day. That final morning, two unhappy creatures walked into my office, not one.

It was time. She didn't say a thing. She just fell asleep, and the last thing she heard was how much she was loved as I kissed her forehead for you.

Be encouraged,

Dr. Jack

A dog's best friend is his illiteracy.

—Ogden Nash

Opie

$\mathcal{D}$ear Mr. and Mrs. Hays and kids,

There are not a lot of Opies in the world. That dog could have been in movies. What a ham. (In fact, he reminded me of Asta, the schnauzer in *The Thin Man*.) At the same time there was nothing but gentleness and love in every hair on that hairy body.

He was the kind of dog that wanted to please, but that's only part of all he was. His family knew him in ways only they know to miss. There was a certain way he would nuzzle with his nose. There was a certain feel to his fur. He had an Opie odor about him, not offensive, just there. "Just there" . . . that's the hard part, isn't it? There was a presence about him that fit, and now he's lost to senility and incontinence. Without Opie, there's something just not quite right about home.

Maybe I'm going too far with all this, but I don't think so, because I sensed this by knowing him only fifteen minutes a year, and you had him much longer. He was a dog to fall in love with. He had a way of looking at you. I think it was a look of adoration.

Thinking of you,

Dr. Jack

A dog will never forget the crumb thou gavest him, though thou mayst afterwards throw a hundred stones at his head.

—Sa'di

Brugus

Dear Mrs. Flanders,

Brugus was so young, only five years old. Hip dysplasia is devastating for these larger breeds and eventually causes premature end to life. Then to have both his knees ruptured was too much to go through.

Only you know the intimate ways this dog touched your heart, the way he'd tilt his head to look at you, the way he'd smell when he came in from the rain. But we in this office know how much you and Brugus meant to each other, and you can be sure that our thoughts are with you.

Be well,

Dr. Jack

Our dogs will love and
admire the meanest of us,
and feed our colossal vanity
with their uncritical homage.

—Agnes Repplier

Stallone

*D*ear Morgan family,

I love German shepherds. They are a most noble breed of loyal family dogs. That's why this is a sickening and debilitating thing for these dogs to go through. They seem to have everything you could want: looks, intelligence, personality, devotion, strength. And yet so many of them fall prey to spinal degeneration.

I have gone through the same kind of pain you and your family have felt this past week. It seems like the little unexpected things are always reminding us of the big loss. There may be a spot on the floor that was his or a place you would go with him, or an area where you'd have to keep cleaning up his hair (these shepherds shed enough for any ten dogs), and this would conjure up memories of Stallone.

Dogs seem to be the only ones that understand us sometimes. Were you ever sad, and no one else knew, but

Stallone would place his head on your lap and seem to understand just the way you felt? There is nothing else like that connection. And it is the loss of that connection that brings such sadness.

Your grief will get better in time. But in a sense, it's testimony to the greatness of your dog.

One shepherd lover to another,

Dr. Jack

Dogs live with man as courtiers around a monarch.
—Robert Louis Stevenson

Bananas

Dear Mr. Calvis,

There is a first and a last heartbeat, a beginning and an end. Oh, how I wish we could get that first heartbeat back and enjoy the wonder of life when we're young and joints don't hurt, breathing is easy, energy is inexhaustible, and age is for some other time. There must have been a time when Bananas was tireless, bursting with more love than you'd think one golden retriever could hold. They have so much love; it just bursts out of them on us. We people get used to it. And the importance of it doesn't hit us until it's gone.

It probably won't take away the pain of your loss—at least not yet—but I hope you always remember the baker's dozen good years you had with Bananas. Even the time when he was six and we had to take those porcupine quills out of him seems like a sweet memory now, doesn't it?

Geriatric arthritis can't cancel out the good memories; the complications from his anti-inflammatory can't either. We need to let the love of that big old dog be part of your heart now forever—to burst out, overflow, and affect others.

Warmly,

Dr. Jack

They say a reasonable amount o' fleas is good fer a dog keeps him from broodin' over bein' a dog, mebbe.
—Edward Noyes Westcott

Bur Rabbit

*D*ear Mr. Valdosta,

I want to write you a few words in honor of Bur Rabbit. I'm a bit partial to Labs since I owned one once . . . or I should say one owned me. Bur Rabbit was a typical wonderful chocolate goofball. Everyone here knew him by sight and name. He was the last link to your dear wife in your immediate family. Now he is free from painful chemo treatments.

He had a good life, and made yours better. Rejoice for him.

Yours,

Dr. Jack

I need a dog pretty badly.
I dreamed of dogs last night.
They sat in a circle and looked at me
and I wanted all of them.

—John Steinbeck

Huggles

Dear Misses Brainerd,

Huggles was an institution in your family. She was there through untold family changes that brought two sisters back to live together after a lifetime. And two weeks ago, she died peacefully in her sleep, crossing the bridge that all of us someday must cross. Discovering her that morning, I know, was a hard, hard thing for you, Miss Anna.

I'd like to think that in her deepest thoughts she started across that bridge an old dog, unable to walk without pain. Then she heard your voices telling her how much you loved her, and started walking a little faster. Perhaps there was a lightness to her step that hadn't been there for years, and breathing was easier. She began to smell the fragrance of eternity. Glancing back, she missed you, but there was a sense of completeness. She knew she could go on and all was well. At the end of that bridge, she was young again. She ran full speed into the field of beauty that lay before her, and her back legs, no longer in their K-9 cart, almost outran her front. Then she thought of you again, and two words filled her heart, *Thank you.*

Respectfully,

Dr. Jack

Let dogs delight to bark and bite,
For God hath made them so.
—Isaac Watts

Baron

Dear Mr. Okun,

Baron had a big personality; he was immense in presence. I looked forward to seeing this good-looking Rottweiler whenever I saw him scheduled. We had a unique relationship. He wanted to like me, but at the same time he needed to keep his territorial edge. Thankfully his dad was always there to referee. Baron didn't accept a lot of people, so I always felt honored that he saw fit to include me in his acceptable but guarded relationships.

In the three weeks since your loss, I hope the pain of losing Baron has been accompanied by good memories of him. I know he was your best buddy. When I lost my dog to cancer, it took me about six months to get to the point where I wouldn't cry every time I thought of her.

Sometimes things seem to come on suddenly, but in reality have been brewing underneath the surface for some time. That's the way it is with cancer. Baron was a strong, tough dog, but being strong and tough doesn't mean anything when your own body turns against you.

I just want you to know you have plenty of company and we all share in your sadness.

Sincerely,

Dr. Jack

Like human babies, puppies even smell special.
—Gina Spadafori

Sanford

Dear Mr. and Mrs. Strait,

I'm writing you because it fell upon me to walk Sanford through his last minutes. Sanford was brought to me in the treatment room unable to walk or to control his urine. He didn't cry, though I'm sure he was in pain. He seemed to understand that all would soon be okay. He seemed unusually calm. We gave him hugs and told him what a good boy he was. He had dignity, and rested all in peace.

Be encouraged,

Dr. Jack

Inside every Newfoundland,
Boxer, Elkhound, and Great
Dane is a puppy longing to
climb into your lap.

—Hellen Thomson

Hazey

Dear Ms. Englander,

You and I have been through this before. As we discussed, because of your calling as a rescuer of stray dogs, this probably won't be the last time. Hazey came to you with dislocations, heart problems, kidney problems, and more, and not once did you shrink from caring for her. Only when it became evident that she could never have a quality life again did you let her go.

When I think about the way your sister in her wheelchair depended on you before MS finally took her, and the way Hazey depended on you, I understand that we have little control over our circumstances. We're each made with certain qualities and gifts, and we are who we are. Can clay say to the potter who formed it, "I should be a different vase"? It isn't the clay that is in control, it's the potter. All the vase can do is exist in its proper form—and you are a beautiful vase. So I'll keep the tissues handy, and you keep doing what you do, and together we'll make sure that we're good stewards of all the furry creatures placed in our care.

Take courage,

Dr. Jack

To his dog, every man is Napoleon.

—Aldous Huxley

Madge

Dear Miss Ferro,

I wish I could write something profound that would remove your heartache concerning Madge. I wish I could explain exactly how it all has purpose and meaning. Our perspective on things is so small, and asking the question "Why" often leads to frustration.

Madge was a classic beauty, strictly collie. When she had her pups, we were all rooting for her. She already showed signs of hormonal imbalance, and had a history of miscarriage. Tragically, both pups were born with heart valve problems, and lived only weeks.

I've enclosed a copy of Madge's blood work to show you how catastrophic her illness was. She suffered from a combination of adrenal disease and diabetes. I still think her heart was abnormal as well—only her physical heart, that is, for her emotional heart was as strong as could be. Madge's final crisis came on suddenly, and who knows, maybe she almost wished it so.

You were a good, attentive friend to Madge. I hope your time of grief and that of her furry housemates will be short. Console one another and cherish the time you have. Hug all of your animals and let them know how much you love them. The return on invested love is magnificent.

With heartfelt condolences,

Dr. Jack

The dog . . . commends himself to our favor by affording play to our propensity for mastery.
—Thorstein Veblen

Peppermint

$\mathcal{D}$ear Reagan,

Peppermint was your first dog, and there are so many things you must miss. Her smell, her warmth, the way she'd look at you—but most of all the way she loved you. You could be in any mood, look any way, say anything, and it didn't matter. To her, you didn't have to prove anything. She accepted you just as you are. Nowhere else does that kind of love exist with that kind of consistency. Be brave and thankful.

Regards to Mom and Dad,

Dr. Jack

No civilization is complete
which does not include the
dumb and defenseless of
God's creatures within
the sphere of charity and
mercy.

—Queen Victoria

O' Ryan

Dear Mr. and Mrs. Connolly,

This week I lost a good little friend. Whenever O'Ryan would come into the clinic, she had a way of making everything around her more joyful. She was small for a Shetland, but her spirit was huge. When she wagged her tail (or I should say stump), her whole rear end would shimmy. She had a way of making you feel included in her world.

When she first came here, she weighed all of three pounds. Little did you know it would be the first of many visits to the vet. Even after total ear ablation causing complete deafness, she would come in and trot confidently to the exam room, treatment rooms, and other areas almost on her own. She knew this place well. She learned how to understand a sign language of sorts, so her deafness didn't seem to handicap her much. And even through all the medical and surgical treatments, she remained eager to please.

I know you both have so much more in memories. You went to bat for her more times than we could count. But because of all she was, she was worth it. Thank you for being such good parents.

Warmly,

Dr. Jack

Dogs got personality. Personality goes a long way.

—Quentin Tarantino
and Roger Avary

Bambie

*D*ear Mrs. Blake-Ward,

It was a week ago that we had to say good-bye to
Bambie. She was the perfect dog for your family for six-
teen years, though she did rule the roost in some ways.
The way she would shake her food bowl and be an occa-
sional butt-nipper just a couple of things that set her
apart. Obviously an excellent protector, that Old English
sheepdog was a living, breathing, pulsing, infinitely
patient piece of play equipment for your kids.

It amazes me how our canine friends affect our lives
on so many different levels. Our dogs seem to be tailored
for each separate member of a family, forging a different
relationship with each human in the household. Bambie
was gifted at loving each of you in a special way.
Certainly the children in your family have had to suffer
a tremendous loss, having never known life without

Bambie. I know that each of you has your own memories and your own heartache to encounter.

Sometimes when we're going through the pain of loss, it can feel very lonely. But rest assured, all of us who have ever loved and lost an animal are with you during this time.

With warm memories,

Dr. Jack

Dogs often remind us of the human, all-too-human. Cats, never.

—Mason Cooley

LadyBlain

*D*ear Miss Ruskin,

The pain of losing LadyBlain is testimony to the great and beautiful love of a dog who could sense the secret places of your heart. There are times in our lives when we don't even know we need healing. Sometimes we experience pain for so long, we begin to think it's normal. She appeared not to remove the pain but simply to be present with you. She was your source of unconditional love. How fortunate you were in having her.

Sincerely,

Dr. Jack

*Histories are more full of
examples of the fidelity of dogs
than of friends.*

—Alexander Pope

Plato

Dear Mr. and Mrs. Gristede,

Plato was in the midst of emotional turmoil and unhappiness most of his life. This was a mental illness and it was progressive. After your move to a new home, his whole world was devastated. The simplest thing became a challenge to him. He could not stand on his own. The slightest noise would terrify him. He would cope with that by destructive behavior. Violence was a pacifier to him and was not meanness or retribution. He loved you deeply and was never angry with you for leaving him alone during your working hours.

As I look at his record and see him as a nine-pound pup on his first visit to us, it is disheartening to think how such a cute creature with all the attention he got from you could ever come to this end. It is a tragedy. But there is no doubt in my heart that you did the right thing in deciding to spare him a miserable decline. He was already suffering greatly.

You laid down a part of your lives for Plato, and it's now time to pick up that fragment and go on to a new day and good things to come.

Take heart,

Dr. Jack

Dogs are indeed the most social, affectionate, and amiable animals of t he whole brute creation.
—Edmund Burke

Zeb

 *D*ear Jason and Helen,

It seems so unfair that Zeb in his youth would give in to such a silly temptation as eating pennies. After all, chewing on coins sounds harmless enough and even comical. But harmful things that seem harmless at the time can befall any of us—and Bedlington terriers are especially genetically susceptible to copper toxicosis.

I was hoping beyond hope that maybe by some miracle Zeb would get better, even though we all knew how poor the prognosis was. But there are a few things I want to say in this letter. Number one, you were good parents to Zeb. You know how to raise a dog. Look at all the other dogs you've had in the past and how long they lived. Number two, no one knew Zeb was eating pennies till it was too late. Number three, even if he did have the surgery and blood transfusion, his chances of survival were very small. You are not ever, ever to blame yourself for not having the money to proceed with surgery. Not having money is not a sin—not having enough heart and compassion is. You had enough heart for any twelve people that last day with Zeb.

Yours sincerely,

Dr. Jack

In order to really enjoy a dog, one doesn't merely try to train him to be semihuman. The point of it is to open oneself to the possibility of becoming partly a dog.
—Edward Hoagland

Duke

*D*ear Mason family,

I would like to write a few words in Duke's memory. He made it to fourteen, a ripe age for a shepherd cross, especially when he had a rough start. He had hip joint surgery more than a decade ago, probably hit by a car. From then on, he was here often. Unfortunately, the last few visits brought news of eventual kidney failure. The final visit is always the hardest. You were good to him that day and throughout his life.

Take care,

Dr. Jack

A dog will make eye contact . . .
A dog will look at you as if to say,
"What do you want me to do for you?
I'll do anything for you." . . .
The dog is willing.

—Roy Blount Jr.

Trixy

*D*ear Ms. Motherwell,

I hope all went well with Trixy's burial. I hope you included some of her personal things to go with her. And I hope the pain of loss will be replaced by the joy of memory.

Let me tell you a story: Once, I knew a dog who used to come in with one of our technicians. Every day that dog would wangle a cookie out of the cookie jar on the front office counter. She'd come in, sit down, and stare up at that jar until someone gave her a cookie. One morning she came in, sat down, stared, and nothing happened. She could see the jar, but someone had taken all her cookies. She sat there gazing in unbelief at an empty jar.

We get used to things in life, then one day we wake up and find someone stole all our cookies. We sit there staring in wonder at our empty jar.

Trixy, your Irish setter, was some cookie. She was sleek, smart, and sociable—a secret and a proclamation in one, a walking masterpiece, and a friend of your heart. I know how much you gave each other. I know the pain of your loss.

Be encouraged,

Dr. Jack

You call to a dog and the dog
will break its neck to get to you.
Dogs just want to please.
—Lewis Grizzard

Jax

Dear Mr. and Mrs. Fellowes,

I was on vacation last week, so I just heard about Jax. He was in for a nail trim only a week before his sudden heart attack. It's amazing to me how things happen.

Jax first came to us twelve years ago with ear problems. Obviously he read the book on spaniels and was doing the Brittany spaniel ear-problem thing. Eleven years ago he had callus on his elbows. Ten years ago he lost his anal sacs and also went to the emergency clinic for bite wounds. He decided to get warts six years ago. From then on, it was a little of this and a little of that. Sometimes he'd stay with us a few days. He'd rest in his "hotel room," waiting for your return and dreaming of hunting, I'm sure—dreaming about grass smells, bird smells, water smells, and running like the wind. What a great dog. I had an English setter, so I'm a little partial to the sporting breeds. Jax was a gentle giant who lived a long life for his breed. Now his dreams are forever; your friend, my namesake, is young again.

There is no way to convey how unbelievably special these dogs become in our lives.

Take heart,

Dr. Jack

You learn not to discipline your dogs when you are mad, and that is most of the time when you are disciplining dogs.
—Lou Schultz

Ricki

Dear Mr. and Mrs. Alston and family,

Ricki was a light wherever she went, and her lack of eyesight never slowed her down. That cuddly Shih-Tzu gave laughter with her antics, joy with her presence, warmth in her desire for closeness. There are so many lives that are affected by the life of a dog (although I'm not sure about her knowing she was a dog). And I'm sure she affected all of you in very special and personal ways. Ricki's time had come, but she's there for you to visit anytime you want. Just close your eyes and call.

Be strong,

Dr. Jack

A good snow machine will cost $2,000 and last four or five years. With dogs, you've got regenerative powers. Snow machines don't have puppies.

—Lou Schultz,
trainer of Alaskan huskies

Midnight

Dear Gregor,

How bottomless is the grief we experienced today, when we said farewell to our dear friend Midnight. She was many things: a playgirl, a confidante, a partner in crime, a people trainer (she knew how to get what she wanted from me), and a lady. In one short moment we were with her, and then in the next we were without her. No one has to tell you that you were a good dad to her. At your kennel, you've had as much experience with dogs as I've had.

She was able to live almost seven good quality months after the removal of her mammary tumor. She seemed to bounce back from everything during her active life, but there's no bouncing back from metastatic cancer. I asked you if you wanted to stay present with her during her passing. I'll not forget your answer: "She has stood by me all these years, it's time for me to stand by her."

There are defining moments when courage and fear, happiness and sadness, loss and hope all coexist. All of us in that room were in unity sharing and celebrating a life process. I'm glad we all were with her.

In friendship,

Dr. Jack

The behavior of men to the lower animals, and their behavior to each other, bear a constant relationship.

—Herbert Spencer

Homeboy

Dear Sergeant Young,

There is nothing more moving than an officer of the law carrying his best friend into the hospital for their last good-bye. Homeboy at one time could outrun any suspect, and jump and tackle with the strength of ten. He had the look of shepherd generations. It was what his father and his father's father were bred to do—and you'd best not leave him at home. He lived to ride. In that car, with lights and noise and the sounds of the city, every radio call was for him. If he saw his master looking to the left and right, he was doing the same, ears forward, face set in anticipation.

In old age, the desire was still there, but anemia sapped his stamina. In place of a strong, sleek frame, last week there was little more than a bony prominence under a matted coat of fur. You carried him in a blue blanket and laid him on the exam table. When I laid hands on his fur I knew. That wasn't Homeboy.

Just one more time was all he wanted. Just to smell the seats, to steady himself around corners, to hear the siren.

Rest in honor, Homeboy.

Sincerely,

Dr. Jack

He that wrongs any creature sins against God, the Creator.

—Benjamin Whichcote

Menace

Dear Mrs. Pine,

When a dog as old as Menace comes here, I know the immensity of my task. There is no replacement for a beloved pet, but the love and good they work in us outlast them.

You mentioned your grandkids wondering what they were going to do without Menace. The answer is they will grow, and growing is often painful. Perhaps this loss has even brought you all closer. The importance of animals in our lives is greater than we know.

Be of good heart,

Dr. Jack

The higher animals are in a sense drawn into Man when he loves them and makes them (as he does) much more nearly human than they would otherwise be.

—C. S. Lewis

I'll always remember you...

_____

(Dog's name)

Nickname _____

Born _____

(Month, day, year)

Died _____

(Month, day, year)

Parent(s) _____

Affix snapshot here.

I'll always remember you...

Special memories: _____

_____

_____

_____

Endearing behavior: _____

_____

_____

_____

Favorite foods: _____

_____

_____

_____

Favorite games: _____

_____

_____ _____

_____ _____

I'll always remember you...

_____

_____

_____

_____

_____

_____

_____

_____

_____

_____

_____

_____

The dog is mentioned in the Bible
eighteen times—the cat not even once.
—W. E. Farbstein

I still miss you...

rest now in peace.

Good-bye, My Faithful Friend.